THIS BOOK BELONGS TO:

CONTACT INFORMATION	
NAME:	
ADDRESS:	
PHONE:	

START / END DATES

___ / ___ / ___   TO   ___ / ___ / ___

DEDICATION

This Trading Journal log is dedicated to all the investors out there who want to track all of their trades and document their findings in the process.

You are my inspiration for producing books and I'm honored to be a part of keeping all of your trading notes and records organized.

This journal notebook will help you record your details about your trades.

Thoughtfully put together with these sections to record:

Date, Time, Currency Pair, Sell/ Buy, Lot Size, # of Trades Placed, PIP Gain, How Long?, Strategy Used, Trends Noticed, & Notes.

HOW TO USE THIS BOOK

The purpose of this book is to keep all of your trading notes all in one place. It will help keep you organized.

This Trading Journal will allow you to accurately document every detail about your trades. It's a great way to chart your course through recording your trading activities.

Here are examples of the prompts for you to fill in and write about your experience in this book:

1. Date - Log the date of your trade.

2. Time - Record the time of your trade.

3. Currency Pair - Write the quotation for different currencies.

4. Sell/ Buy - Log whether you plan to buy or sell and price.

5. Lot Size - Record the lot size.

6. Number Of Trades Placed - Write the # of trades you made.

7. PIP Gain - Log the Point in Percentage gain.

8. How Long? - Record how long you plan to hold.

9. Strategy Used - Write the strategy or strategies you used, swing, position, etc.

10. Trends Noticed - Log any trends you may see.

11. Notes - For writing any important information you want such as notes on market conditions, profit targets, stops, trading rules, future plans & goals, and more.

TRADING JOURNAL

DATE	TIME	CURRENCY PAIR	SELL/BUY	LOT SIZE	# OF TRADES PLACED	PIP GAIN	HOW LONG?	STRATEGY USED

TRADING JOURNAL

DATE	TIME	CURRENCY PAIR	SELL/BUY	LOT SIZE	# OF TRADES PLACED	PIP GAIN	HOW LONG?	STRATEGY USED

TRENDS NOTICED

NOTES

TRADING JOURNAL

DATE	TIME	CURRENCY PAIR	SELL/BUY	LOT SIZE	# OF TRADES PLACED	PIP GAIN	HOW LONG?	STRATEGY USED

TRADING JOURNAL

DATE	TIME	CURRENCY PAIR	SELL/BUY	LOT SIZE	# OF TRADES PLACED	PIP GAIN	HOW LONG?	STRATEGY USED

TRADING JOURNAL

DATE	TIME	CURRENCY PAIR	SELL/BUY	LOT SIZE	# OF TRADES PLACED	PIP GAIN	HOW LONG?	STRATEGY USED

TRENDS NOTICED

NOTES

TRADING JOURNAL

DATE	TIME	CURRENCY PAIR	SELL/BUY	LOT SIZE	# OF TRADES PLACED	PIP GAIN	HOW LONG?	STRATEGY USED

TRADING JOURNAL

DATE	TIME	CURRENCY PAIR	SELL/BUY	LOT SIZE	# OF TRADES PLACED	PIP GAIN	HOW LONG?	STRATEGY USED

TRADING JOURNAL

DATE	TIME	CURRENCY PAIR	SELL/BUY	LOT SIZE	# OF TRADES PLACED	PIP GAIN	HOW LONG?	STRATEGY USED

TRADING JOURNAL

DATE	TIME	CURRENCY PAIR	SELL/BUY	LOT SIZE	# OF TRADES PLACED	PIP GAIN	HOW LONG?	STRATEGY USED

TRADING JOURNAL

DATE	TIME	CURRENCY PAIR	SELL/BUY	LOT SIZE	# OF TRADES PLACED	PIP GAIN	HOW LONG?	STRATEGY USED

TRENDS NOTICED

NOTES

TRADING JOURNAL

DATE	TIME	CURRENCY PAIR	SELL/BUY	LOT SIZE	# OF TRADES PLACED	PIP GAIN	HOW LONG?	STRATEGY USED

TRADING JOURNAL

DATE	TIME	CURRENCY PAIR	SELL/BUY	LOT SIZE	# OF TRADES PLACED	PIP GAIN	HOW LONG?	STRATEGY USED

TRENDS NOTICED   NOTES

TRADING JOURNAL

DATE	TIME	CURRENCY PAIR	SELL/BUY	LOT SIZE	# OF TRADES PLACED	PIP GAIN	HOW LONG?	STRATEGY USED

TRADING JOURNAL

DATE	TIME	CURRENCY PAIR	SELL/BUY	LOT SIZE	# OF TRADES PLACED	PIP GAIN	HOW LONG?	STRATEGY USED

TRADING JOURNAL

DATE	TIME	CURRENCY PAIR	SELL/BUY	LOT SIZE	# OF TRADES PLACED	PIP GAIN	HOW LONG?	STRATEGY USED

TRENDS NOTICED   NOTES

TRADING JOURNAL

DATE	TIME	CURRENCY PAIR	SELL/BUY	LOT SIZE	# OF TRADES PLACED	PIP GAIN	HOW LONG?	STRATEGY USED

TRADING JOURNAL

DATE	TIME	CURRENCY PAIR	SELL/BUY	LOT SIZE	# OF TRADES PLACED	PIP GAIN	HOW LONG?	STRATEGY USED

TRENDS NOTICED

NOTES

TRADING JOURNAL

DATE	TIME	CURRENCY PAIR	SELL/BUY	LOT SIZE	# OF TRADES PLACED	PIP GAIN	HOW LONG?	STRATEGY USED

TRADING JOURNAL

DATE	TIME	CURRENCY PAIR	SELL/BUY	LOT SIZE	# OF TRADES PLACED	PIP GAIN	HOW LONG?	STRATEGY USED

TRENDS NOTICED

NOTES

TRADING JOURNAL

DATE	TIME	CURRENCY PAIR	SELL/BUY	LOT SIZE	# OF TRADES PLACED	PIP GAIN	HOW LONG?	STRATEGY USED

TRADING JOURNAL

DATE	TIME	CURRENCY PAIR	SELL/BUY	LOT SIZE	# OF TRADES PLACED	PIP GAIN	HOW LONG?	STRATEGY USED

TRADING JOURNAL

DATE	TIME	CURRENCY PAIR	SELL/BUY	LOT SIZE	# OF TRADES PLACED	PIP GAIN	HOW LONG?	STRATEGY USED

TRADING JOURNAL

DATE	TIME	CURRENCY PAIR	SELL/BUY	LOT SIZE	# OF TRADES PLACED	PIP GAIN	HOW LONG?	STRATEGY USED

TRENDS NOTICED

NOTES

TRADING JOURNAL

DATE	TIME	CURRENCY PAIR	SELL/BUY	LOT SIZE	# OF TRADES PLACED	PIP GAIN	HOW LONG?	STRATEGY USED

TRADING JOURNAL

DATE	TIME	CURRENCY PAIR	SELL/BUY	LOT SIZE	# OF TRADES PLACED	PIP GAIN	HOW LONG?	STRATEGY USED

TRENDS NOTICED   NOTES

TRADING JOURNAL

DATE	TIME	CURRENCY PAIR	SELL/BUY	LOT SIZE	# OF TRADES PLACED	PIP GAIN	HOW LONG?	STRATEGY USED

TRENDS NOTICED

NOTES

TRADING JOURNAL

DATE	TIME	CURRENCY PAIR	SELL/BUY	LOT SIZE	# OF TRADES PLACED	PIP GAIN	HOW LONG?	STRATEGY USED

TRADING JOURNAL

DATE	TIME	CURRENCY PAIR	SELL/BUY	LOT SIZE	# OF TRADES PLACED	PIP GAIN	HOW LONG?	STRATEGY USED

TRADING JOURNAL

DATE	TIME	CURRENCY PAIR	SELL/BUY	LOT SIZE	# OF TRADES PLACED	PIP GAIN	HOW LONG?	STRATEGY USED

TRENDS NOTICED   NOTES

TRADING JOURNAL

DATE	TIME	CURRENCY PAIR	SELL/BUY	LOT SIZE	# OF TRADES PLACED	PIP GAIN	HOW LONG?	STRATEGY USED

TRADING JOURNAL

DATE	TIME	CURRENCY PAIR	SELL/BUY	LOT SIZE	# OF TRADES PLACED	PIP GAIN	HOW LONG?	STRATEGY USED

TRENDS NOTICED   NOTES

TRADING JOURNAL

DATE	TIME	CURRENCY PAIR	SELL/BUY	LOT SIZE	# OF TRADES PLACED	PIP GAIN	HOW LONG?	STRATEGY USED

TRADING JOURNAL

DATE	TIME	CURRENCY PAIR	SELL/BUY	LOT SIZE	# OF TRADES PLACED	PIP GAIN	HOW LONG?	STRATEGY USED

TRADING JOURNAL

DATE	TIME	CURRENCY PAIR	SELL/BUY	LOT SIZE	# OF TRADES PLACED	PIP GAIN	HOW LONG?	STRATEGY USED

TRENDS NOTICED

NOTES

TRADING JOURNAL

DATE	TIME	CURRENCY PAIR	SELL/BUY	LOT SIZE	# OF TRADES PLACED	PIP GAIN	HOW LONG?	STRATEGY USED

TRADING JOURNAL

DATE	TIME	CURRENCY PAIR	SELL/BUY	LOT SIZE	# OF TRADES PLACED	PIP GAIN	HOW LONG?	STRATEGY USED

TRADING JOURNAL

DATE	TIME	CURRENCY PAIR	SELL/BUY	LOT SIZE	# OF TRADES PLACED	PIP GAIN	HOW LONG?	STRATEGY USED

TRENDS NOTICED

NOTES

TRADING JOURNAL

DATE	TIME	CURRENCY PAIR	SELL/BUY	LOT SIZE	# OF TRADES PLACED	PIP GAIN	HOW LONG?	STRATEGY USED

TRENDS NOTICED   NOTES

TRADING JOURNAL

DATE	TIME	CURRENCY PAIR	SELL/BUY	LOT SIZE	# OF TRADES PLACED	PIP GAIN	HOW LONG?	STRATEGY USED

TRENDS NOTICED

NOTES

TRADING JOURNAL

DATE	TIME	CURRENCY PAIR	SELL/BUY	LOT SIZE	# OF TRADES PLACED	PIP GAIN	HOW LONG?	STRATEGY USED

TRADING JOURNAL

DATE	TIME	CURRENCY PAIR	SELL/BUY	LOT SIZE	# OF TRADES PLACED	PIP GAIN	HOW LONG?	STRATEGY USED

TRENDS NOTICED   NOTES

TRADING JOURNAL

DATE	TIME	CURRENCY PAIR	SELL/BUY	LOT SIZE	# OF TRADES PLACED	PIP GAIN	HOW LONG?	STRATEGY USED

TRADING JOURNAL

DATE	TIME	CURRENCY PAIR	SELL/BUY	LOT SIZE	# OF TRADES PLACED	PIP GAIN	HOW LONG?	STRATEGY USED

TRADING JOURNAL

DATE	TIME	CURRENCY PAIR	SELL/BUY	LOT SIZE	# OF TRADES PLACED	PIP GAIN	HOW LONG?	STRATEGY USED

TRADING JOURNAL

DATE	TIME	CURRENCY PAIR	SELL/BUY	LOT SIZE	# OF TRADES PLACED	PIP GAIN	HOW LONG?	STRATEGY USED

TRENDS NOTICED   NOTES

TRADING JOURNAL

DATE	TIME	CURRENCY PAIR	SELL/BUY	LOT SIZE	# OF TRADES PLACED	PIP GAIN	HOW LONG?	STRATEGY USED

TRADING JOURNAL

DATE	TIME	CURRENCY PAIR	SELL/BUY	LOT SIZE	# OF TRADES PLACED	PIP GAIN	HOW LONG?	STRATEGY USED

TRENDS NOTICED

NOTES

TRADING JOURNAL

DATE	TIME	CURRENCY PAIR	SELL/BUY	LOT SIZE	# OF TRADES PLACED	PIP GAIN	HOW LONG?	STRATEGY USED

TRADING JOURNAL

DATE	TIME	CURRENCY PAIR	SELL/BUY	LOT SIZE	# OF TRADES PLACED	PIP GAIN	HOW LONG?	STRATEGY USED

TRADING JOURNAL

DATE	TIME	CURRENCY PAIR	SELL/BUY	LOT SIZE	# OF TRADES PLACED	PIP GAIN	HOW LONG?	STRATEGY USED

TRADING JOURNAL

DATE	TIME	CURRENCY PAIR	SELL/BUY	LOT SIZE	# OF TRADES PLACED	PIP GAIN	HOW LONG?	STRATEGY USED

TRADING JOURNAL

DATE	TIME	CURRENCY PAIR	SELL/BUY	LOT SIZE	# OF TRADES PLACED	PIP GAIN	HOW LONG?	STRATEGY USED

TRENDS NOTICED   NOTES

TRADING JOURNAL

DATE	TIME	CURRENCY PAIR	SELL/BUY	LOT SIZE	# OF TRADES PLACED	PIP GAIN	HOW LONG?	STRATEGY USED

TRENDS NOTICED

NOTES

TRADING JOURNAL

DATE	TIME	CURRENCY PAIR	SELL/BUY	LOT SIZE	# OF TRADES PLACED	PIP GAIN	HOW LONG?	STRATEGY USED

TRENDS NOTICED   NOTES

TRADING JOURNAL

DATE	TIME	CURRENCY PAIR	SELL/BUY	LOT SIZE	# OF TRADES PLACED	PIP GAIN	HOW LONG?	STRATEGY USED

TRADING JOURNAL

DATE	TIME	CURRENCY PAIR	SELL/BUY	LOT SIZE	# OF TRADES PLACED	PIP GAIN	HOW LONG?	STRATEGY USED

TRADING JOURNAL

DATE	TIME	CURRENCY PAIR	SELL/BUY	LOT SIZE	# OF TRADES PLACED	PIP GAIN	HOW LONG?	STRATEGY USED

TRADING JOURNAL

DATE	TIME	CURRENCY PAIR	SELL/BUY	LOT SIZE	# OF TRADES PLACED	PIP GAIN	HOW LONG?	STRATEGY USED

TRENDS NOTICED   NOTES

TRADING JOURNAL

DATE	TIME	CURRENCY PAIR	SELL/BUY	LOT SIZE	# OF TRADES PLACED	PIP GAIN	HOW LONG?	STRATEGY USED

TRENDS NOTICED

NOTES

TRADING JOURNAL

DATE	TIME	CURRENCY PAIR	SELL/BUY	LOT SIZE	# OF TRADES PLACED	PIP GAIN	HOW LONG?	STRATEGY USED

TRADING JOURNAL

DATE	TIME	CURRENCY PAIR	SELL/BUY	LOT SIZE	# OF TRADES PLACED	PIP GAIN	HOW LONG?	STRATEGY USED

TRADING JOURNAL

DATE	TIME	CURRENCY PAIR	SELL/BUY	LOT SIZE	# OF TRADES PLACED	PIP GAIN	HOW LONG?	STRATEGY USED

TRADING JOURNAL

DATE	TIME	CURRENCY PAIR	SELL/BUY	LOT SIZE	# OF TRADES PLACED	PIP GAIN	HOW LONG?	STRATEGY USED

TRADING JOURNAL

DATE	TIME	CURRENCY PAIR	SELL/BUY	LOT SIZE	# OF TRADES PLACED	PIP GAIN	HOW LONG?	STRATEGY USED

TRADING JOURNAL

DATE	TIME	CURRENCY PAIR	SELL/BUY	LOT SIZE	# OF TRADES PLACED	PIP GAIN	HOW LONG?	STRATEGY USED

TRADING JOURNAL

DATE	TIME	CURRENCY PAIR	SELL/BUY	LOT SIZE	# OF TRADES PLACED	PIP GAIN	HOW LONG?	STRATEGY USED

TRADING JOURNAL

DATE	TIME	CURRENCY PAIR	SELL/BUY	LOT SIZE	# OF TRADES PLACED	PIP GAIN	HOW LONG?	STRATEGY USED

TRADING JOURNAL

DATE	TIME	CURRENCY PAIR	SELL/BUY	LOT SIZE	# OF TRADES PLACED	PIP GAIN	HOW LONG?	STRATEGY USED

TRADING JOURNAL

DATE	TIME	CURRENCY PAIR	SELL/BUY	LOT SIZE	# OF TRADES PLACED	PIP GAIN	HOW LONG?	STRATEGY USED

TRADING JOURNAL

DATE	TIME	CURRENCY PAIR	SELL/BUY	LOT SIZE	# OF TRADES PLACED	PIP GAIN	HOW LONG?	STRATEGY USED

TRADING JOURNAL

DATE	TIME	CURRENCY PAIR	SELL/BUY	LOT SIZE	# OF TRADES PLACED	PIP GAIN	HOW LONG?	STRATEGY USED

TRADING JOURNAL

DATE	TIME	CURRENCY PAIR	SELL/BUY	LOT SIZE	# OF TRADES PLACED	PIP GAIN	HOW LONG?	STRATEGY USED

TRENDS NOTICED   NOTES

TRADING JOURNAL

DATE	TIME	CURRENCY PAIR	SELL/BUY	LOT SIZE	# OF TRADES PLACED	PIP GAIN	HOW LONG?	STRATEGY USED

TRENDS NOTICED

NOTES

www.ingramcontent.com/pod-product-compliance
Lightning Source LLC
Chambersburg PA
CBHW051756200326
41597CB00025B/4573

* 9 7 8 1 6 4 9 4 4 2 0 4 8 *